The Little Angel Books Series

Color Me One

Written & Illustrated

by Leia A. Stinnett

ISBN 0-929385-82-9

Published by

StarChild Press

a division of
Light Technology
Publishing
P.O. Box 1526
Sedona, Arizona 86339

Printed by

MISSION POSSIBLE
Commercial
Printing

P.O. Box 1495
Sedona, AZ 86339

Color Me One

When the Earth was new, there was but one land that stretched all the way around the world.

Above and below the land, in the areas we now call the North and South Poles, were great bodies of water.

This land was very special. God wanted it to be perfect in every way, reflecting His/Her beauty, joy and love. Thus the land was covered with beautiful trees, flowering plants, animals, golden butterflies and birds of all varieties. This land was the home of the great bird of paradise, a large, colorful bird with long, flowing tail feathers reflecting every color of the rainbow.

Majestic mountains and clear,

bubbling streams dotted the landscape. Everywhere one looked there was beauty . . . and love.

Creator wanted this world to always be a special place of love. So Creator asked some very special angel helpers to come to Earth and watch over the land. In exchange for caring for the Earth and her living things, God promised they would never want for anything . . . ever!

Eagerly, many angels asked to come to Earth for this wonderful After all, they thought, who wouldn't want to live in such a splendid place?

Pleased with the angels' decisions to take care of the Earth, God created for them a happy, colorful garden paradise, where all the angels could live together in love and harmony, equally sharing the chores and the fun.

Creator made certain the garden was filled with everything the angels

could ever possibly want or need to be happy and healthy. God was pleased with His/Her creation. The angels were very pleased as well, and most eager to live in their new home.

Here in this special garden, God's plan was for all the angels to learn to live in harmony with one another – with all the birds, insects, animals, trees, plants and rocks. The angels were to learn that each living thing on Earth had a special purpose in being there, that each was assigned a special role in helping the other stay happy, healthy and strong. The angels were to learn the importance of working hand in hand with nature, rather than against her. They were to learn the importance of sharing equally in God's love and light, the importance of unity, oneness.

Each of the angels had been created equally beautiful in appearance and dress. The angels felt equal – not one angel thought he/she was better than or less than the others.

Because the angels believed they were equal, they did not even notice the difference in their skin colors. All the angels were happy and filled with great joy as they set upon their loving task of watching over and caring for the beautiful Earth.

There was one little angel, however, who just happened one day to be sitting on a rock by the crystal pond. Gazing into the clear water, she was startled to see her reflection, together with the reflection of the many beautifully colored flowers that adorned the garden.

"I'm really not fond of looking like everyone else. I don't think like the others. I don't act like the others. And I'm going to make a change," the little angel thought.

Suddenly she remembered God's words, "This garden has been created as a place of beauty and peace for each of you to enjoy equally."

"The garden provides all you will ever need to be happy and healthy. The animals, birds and the tiny insects are your friends. The beautiful plants, trees, flowers, rocks and crystals are here to bring you joy and love, as well as companionship."

"Enjoy the beauty. Honor each living thing for its importance to you and the Earth. Be happy!"

"But I am *not* happy," the little angel pouted out loud. "God said this garden was here for all of us to enjoy. Ah-ha! I want to be different. I want to be noticed, to stand out in the crowd. I don't want to look like everyone else!"

"I am sure God will understand how I feel. God loves us all equally.

God told us He/She loves us no matter what we feel, think or do. I don't mean anyone else any harm. I just want to be different."

The little angel assured herself that God was busy and not watching her, and that He/She wouldn't mind her taking just one small flower. So she plucked a bright orange flower and attached it to her gown by its stem.

"Oh! That's nice!" she exclaimed as she admired herself in the pond mirror. "I do look different. Now, I *am* happy!"

Three other angels walking near the pond noticed the little girl's adornment. "What did you do to your dress?" the angels asked in unison, surprised at what they saw. They had never considered picking God's beautiful flowers.

"Did you ask permission to pick

that flower?" asked the taller of the three angels.

"Noooo," answered the little angel, looking a bit guilty. "But God said we were to enjoy the garden," she continued defensively. "This is my way of enjoying the garden. It's only one little flower. It won't be missed. Besides, it is so pretty. It makes me feel happy all over when I wear it."

The three angels looked at each other, then at the beautiful row of flowers along the garden path. One by one, they began to sort through the flowers, picking the colors they felt most attracted to.

One angel made a necklace from several flowers and wore it proudly, parading back and forth in front of the other angels, showing off her efforts.

Soon all the angels of the garden were wearing the flowers and comparing each other's creations.

Some angels, in an attempt to out-do the others, decided to search for the *special* flowers – those God warned them were very rare and very important for their health and well-being.

Ignoring Creator's words, the angels tromped through the lush green foliage to find the special flowers, so delicate, so fragile, so perfect, so very beautiful!

Every angel was now trying to out-do the others, to be better than the other angels. The angels were spending all their time competing with one another, ignoring the needs of the garden and the garden's creatures.

Each angel wanted to look better, to be more colorful, more special, to draw more attention than the others. The angels of the wonderful garden had created what we call competition.

No one was happy. The flower

devas were very sad. They did not understand what was happening as all the beautiful flowers were picked one by one, by the very hands chosen to care for them.

Then one day, a very surprised and saddened group of angels discovered all the flowers were gone, as well as all the golden butterflies that had brought them such joy.

The insects, birds and animals were all leaving. There was nothing left for them to eat, no place to sleep. The garden began to wither and die. What was once a place of great joy and happiness now felt lonely and empty.

Watching this fiasco since the first flower was picked, God knew the angels needed to learn a very important lesson.

"So, you want to be different," God said. "You want to look better than one another, different, to wear different colors. No problem!"

God looked around the garden He/She had created for the angels' pleasure. Sadly, Creator exclaimed, "Oh, my! The beautiful garden is no more. Well, my beloved angels, it looks like you will have to find a new home. You must go out into the world in search of a new place to live."

"But can't You fix the garden? Can't You make it as good as new?" pleaded one small angel. "We know You can do anything. We know You can make the garden new."

"Not this time," God responded. "You see, you have lessons to learn here on Earth. It is important that I not interfere with your lessons. I will let you create your own garden. Learn for yourselves what it takes to create a beautiful place in which to live and how to keep it that way.

"It is important for you to learn to

protect what you love. Things change. Once it is gone, it may never again be part of your experience.

"No," God continued, "I will not be able to fix what you have done. But by believing in yourselves, by using the gifts I have given each of you, you can fix it, together.

"When you love each other and all things equally, when you can learn to share, all is possible. Miracles happen when you have faith, when you know I am always with you, no matter where you are, what you are thinking or doing.

"I can best help you create your own garden by allowing you to each stand in your own power, knowing you can do it yourselves. Remember, My loving energy, My power of creation is also a part of you," God said.

The angels hung their heads, feeling a bit ashamed for not caring for the garden as they had agreed to, for picking the beautiful flowers and for creating anything but harmony and balance on the Earth.

But God was *not* angry.

The angels appreciated Creator's understanding. It was all a mistake – a *big* mistake!

Each angel decided to go out into the world and create a garden God would be proud of, to make up for their part in destroying God's wonderful work.

As the angels passed through the gates of the garden in search of a new home, their angel wings disappeared into light. At the same time, the angels suddenly became aware of their differences in color. Some angels were red, some orange; others were yellow and green. Some angels were blue and still others, violet.

The angels felt uncomfortable as

they stopped and stared at each other, not fully understanding what they were feeling about themselves and each other.

So concerned that one color was prettier, better than another, the angels moved into color groups or families. In this way they felt each could support the other based on that particular group's color. They would have to stick together, they felt.

Red angels banded together in search of a new home. Blue angels traveled together looking for a perfect location. Yellow angels formed a group and headed in a different direction, as did the other color groups.

Six different families of angels now traveled across the land, until each color group found a special place on Earth where they felt they could grow the very best garden. After all, the angels did in fact agree on one thing – they all wanted to please God.

The angels carefully searched for the perfect area to build their garden, places where trees, plants and flowers were thriving, where clear, bubbling streams would provide fresh water for new plant life and for the living creatures. The angels wanted so much to be happy once more. God offered loving words of encouragement as the angels learned to love and nurture the devas of the plant, animal and mineral kingdoms. Each day Creator supported their abilities to work more closely with nature and with the special gifts given to each of them.

God knew how important it was for the future of the Earth for the angels to learn how to properly care for and nurture the Earth and her living things, to respect and honor her for giving them what they needed to

live. Yes, this would be a valuable lesson that was to be passed on to future generations of people who would live on the Earth.

For a period of time, all was well on Earth. One day, however, the red angels became curious about what the other angel groups were doing. After all, they thought, they did not want the other groups to have a better garden than they had. They were very proud of their work and knew God was pleased with their accomplishment.

The red angels decided to check out the work of the other angel families. The red angels traveled for several days before encountering another angel family.

The red angels were in awe at the beautiful garden the blue angels had created. There were rainbows and crystals, colorful flowers everywhere, like none they had ever seen before.

The red angels felt the blue angels had created a much better garden than they had. They looked at each other with fire in their eyes.

The red angels marched up to the blue angels. Instead of hugging and loving one another, the red angels attempted to take control, pushing the blue angels out of their garden. The blue angels put up quite a fight to protect their space.

Where was the love now? Where was that special love God had given each of them, to all living things, to the Earth, at the time of creation?

The Earth was experiencing anger, war! All colors of angels were fighting each other. Yellow, green, purple, orange, red and blue angels were pushing, shoving and yelling at one another, picking up plants by their roots, throwing and shattering crystals, stomping on the living things,

Jealousy
Hate!
Anger

destroying each other's homes out of spite, jealousy and not wanting the other to have something better.

The land was covered by a thick blanket of anger, selfishness, feelings of separateness, struggles for power and control. The Earth and all her living things were very sad indeed.

From the conflict and struggle for power, from the hateful, angry energy expressed by the warring angels, the Earth responded in a rumble and roar. Great earthquakes shook the entire planet. The land began to split into large pieces as the angels scrambled in fear.

The angels were frantic, running as fast as they could to return to the areas they had learned to call home before the great waters prevented them from returning.

As the land continued to shake for many days, the land where each angel family had relocated was now separated into a piece surrounded by a large body of water. There was no way the angels could reach each other.

Now they truly were separate – not simply by their colors or feelings, but by the Earth herself. They felt that perhaps even God was not wanting to have anything to do with them. The angels felt very alone.

God had been watching this struggle for power and control. At just the right moment Creator spoke, "So this is what you all want. I let you come to Earth to play, to be happy, to care for a beautiful garden filled with everything you could ever possibly want. And what do you do? You show your appreciation by wanting to be different from each other, separating even from Me. You want to take what the other has because you do not feel your own garden is special enough."

As God spoke, His/Her voice reached all the groups of angels all over the world, and they all paused from what they were doing to listen carefully to what God had to say.

"Look at what you have done," God continued. "Look at the Earth now. By wanting to be better than each other you have caused the Earth much pain. She has separated into pieces to protect herself from more damage.

"When there is no love, no sharing, where there are feelings of separation, greed, selfishness and struggles for power, the Earth cannot survive. Love is the glue that keeps the entire universe together. When you remove the glue – the love – everything falls apart."

"The Earth is no longer in balance. The plants, animals, birds and insects are dying. The Earth herself is dying."

"When they all die, what are you going to do for food and shelter? How are you going to live? Imagine the Earth without any trees, plants, flowers, without the birds, insects or animals . . . only the Sun beating down on a dry, parched Earth without water. What are you going to do?"

Determined to prove Creator wrong, for a short time the angels ignored the warning, thinking only of themselves. They struggled to survive, searching for food and comfortable shelter. Some of the angels were not feeling well and there were no plants left to help them get well.

After a time, one purple angel called a family meeting. "Look at us! None of us are happy. None of us can work together without arguing and picking on each other. It's so difficult now. Remember how wonderful it was in the original garden God made for

LOVE

us? Remember how happy we all were? What happened to us?" the angel asked.

The purple angels all looked at one another. What was missing? They all put their heads together and thought.

What was missing, they decided unanimously, was *love!*

As the angels rediscovered the feeling of love they thought they had lost forever, the love energy went out in waves around the Earth, touching the heart of each of the other angels everywhere. The angels began remembering why they had come to Earth in the first place. The love energy was felt by the Earth and all the living things. Hope was renewed. Maybe, just maybe, the angels could learn to once again live in harmony.

Very pleased with the situation, God smiled and said, "Do not be ashamed, angels. Do not feel guilty or try to hide from Me. I will never punish you. You have learned your lesson well.

"Fill your hearts with love and compassion, with deep concern for each other's well-being. Go now and look for your brother and sister angels. Let the light from your hearts expand and join one with the other into one great light.

"You will once again live in a beautiful garden. This garden will *not* be created by My hands, but from the *love* you now feel inside and from your desire to live in harmony together with the Earth and her living things."

"You have learned your lesson well, angels. You have learned that being separate does not bring you happiness and joy. You have learned that by sharing you can create a new world based on love, harmony and joy, the

way I always intended for you to live on the Earth."

The feelings of love from each angel's heart, and from God's words traveled like waves around the world, reaching the hearts and ears of all the angels everywhere. The angels received special *visions* showing them how to make boats, rafts and bridges by which they could cross the great waters that now separated one group of angels from the other.

The angels vowed that nothing would ever come between them again – nothing. They would not even let their awareness of being different in color, in their feelings and in their actions separate them again.

The angel groups crossed all the barriers that their differences had created. Once again, as brothers and sisters of Creator's family, they joined together, laughing, hugging and crying.

They did not talk about the events that had led to their separation but rather the joy and love they each felt as they came together again.

As the different color groups met, sharing and expanding the love energy in their hearts, their own lights grew brighter and brighter. Reds, oranges, yellows, greens, blues and violets all glowed brighter and began to merge into one great light that beamed out from their bodies, their hearts and shined upward to God.

Surprised, the angels noticed how their different colored lights became one bright white light as they joined together in heart and mind. This great light illuminated their path so brightly they were able to see clearly in the dark of night as they traveled.

"You see, My angels, although you are all different colors, although you may not all think or feel alike, or agree

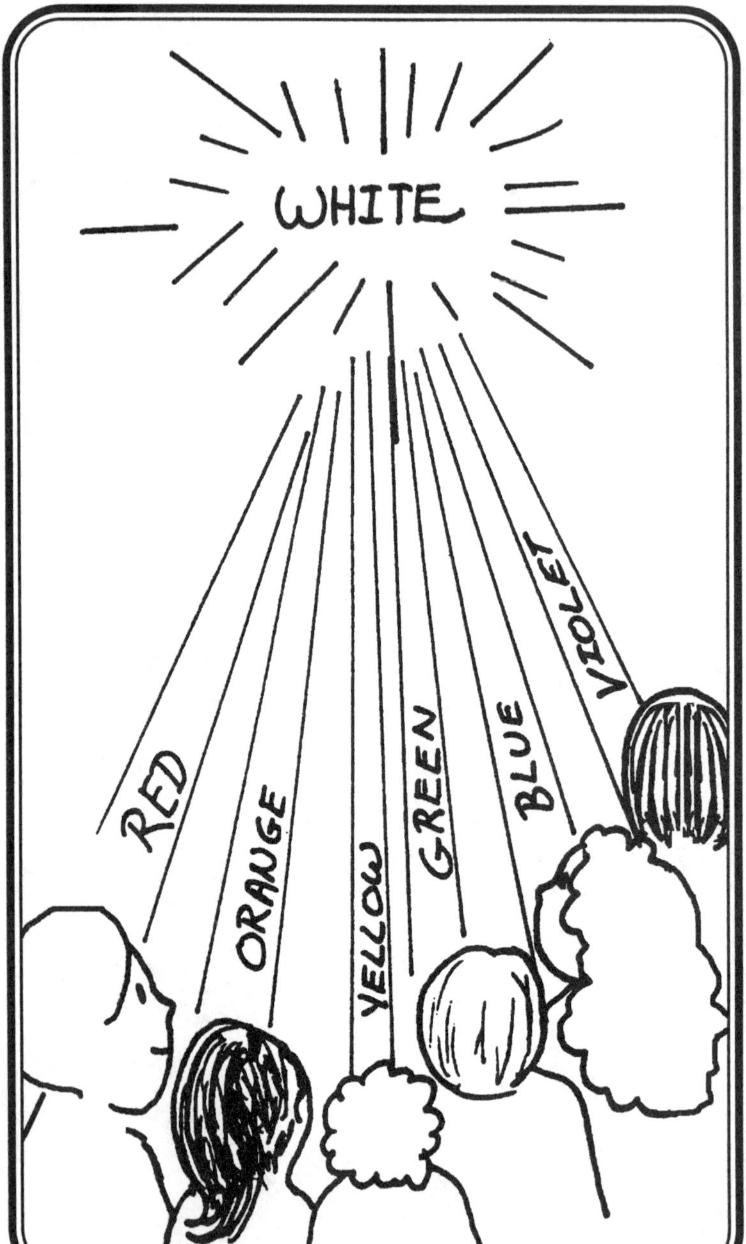
WHITE
RED
ORANGE
YELLOW
GREEN
BLUE
VIOLET

on all things, when you share love among yourselves, when you think of Me and My love for you, you expand your own light. That light is always a part of My light, the great white light from which you came."

"The color white contains all colors. Not one color is more or less important than the rest. If one of your color groups is missing from the larger family, the light will not be as bright."

"Thus, as you see each other as equals, each as important as the other and as a very important part of My light, you will notice the white light growing brighter and stronger. In this light you will feel My love and the love that each of you has for the other angels, for the Earth, for all the living things of creation.

"Here, I will *show* you what I mean. Look at the rainbow over the top of that mountain. See the colors –

red, orange, yellow, green, blue and violet? See how they blend or seem to melt together? If you look closely at the end of the rainbow, you will see all the colors come together as one white light. All the colors together make white.

"Each color looks and feels different. But each color is equally important as part of the white light, just as each of you are equally important in creating the light that I Am.

"You angels made a choice to turn away from My love and support. Look what happened! As you separated from Me, you separated from each other. Instead of being happy, you became lonely and sad."

As the angels worked, Creator reminded them, "One of the laws I created says, whatever you give out unconditionally, unselfishly from your

heart, always comes back to you in a greater amount. As you love the Earth and all living things, as you love yourself, more and more love will come back to you. You will truly be happy, joyful and *free!*

"When you know and accept yourselves as being a part of Me as I am a part of you, when you truly feel My loving presence in all things, in all of creation, and when you can share that love openly with all others, no matter who they are, what they believe, the color of their skin and so on, you will no longer feel separate, alone or unhappy. Where there is love, selfishness, anger, hate and competition cannot exist.

"Remember, angels, we are all one family. The color of your skin made you feel different on the outside, separate from one another. You looked at one another, trying to decide which color was better than the rest. On the inside, in your hearts, there is but one color, one light – the great white light that I Am, that we are together as one family, ever bonded in love.

God smiled as He/She spoke lovingly to the angels of the Earth. The angels looked at one another and smiled, too.

The Earth and all her living things were happy as they once again felt love. Love and peace had once again returned to the Earth. This time, however, the love was stronger than before. The angels learned to appreciate their gifts and the Earth. This time the love was here to stay. All was again in balance and harmony.

God and I Are One

About the Author

The '80s were a decade of self-discovery for Leia Stinnett after she began researching many different avenues of spirituality. In her profession as a graphic designer she had become restless, knowing there was something important she had to do outside the materiality of corporate America.

In August 1986 Leia had her first contact with Archangel Michael when he appeared in a physical form of glowing blue light. A voice said, "I am Michael. Together we will save the children."

In 1988 she was inspired by Michael to teach spiritual classes in Sacramento, California, the Circle of Angels. Through these classes she had the opportunity to work with learning-disabled children, children of abuse and those from dysfunctional homes.

Later Michael told her, "Together we are going to write the Little Angel Books." To date Leia and Michael have created thirteen Little Angel Books that present various topics of spiritual truths and principles. The books proved popular among adults as well as children.

The Circle of Angels classes have been introduced to several countries around the world and across the U.S., and Leia and her husband Douglas now have a teacher's manual and training program for people who wish to offer spiritual classes to children. Leia and Michael have been interviewed on Canadian Satellite TV and have appeared on NBC-TV's *Angels II – Beyond the Light,* which featured their Circle of Angels class and discussed their books and Michael's visit.

The angels have given Leia and Douglas a vision of a new educational system without competition or grades — one that supports love and positive self-esteem, honoring all children as the independent lights they are. Thus they are now writing a curriculum for the new "schools of light" and developing additional books and programs for children.

Other Books by Leia Stinnett:

A Circle of Angels
The Twelve Universal Laws

The Little Angel Books Series:
The Angel Told Me to Tell You Good-bye
The Bridge Between Two Worlds
Crystals R for Kids
Exploring the Chakras
Happy Feet
One Red Rose
When the Earth Was New
Where is God?
Who's Afraid of the Dark?

All My Angel Friends (Coloring Book)